Holistic E

15 Chapters by
Fundamental Information on
Areas of Their Expertise

In this amazing Itty Bitty® book, fifteen practitioners provide you with their expertise on the different systems of the connection of the body mind spirit.

- Winifred Adams - The Secret Behind Medical Intuition
- April Braswell - Soul Essence Love
- Chantalynn - What Makes Your Heart Sing?
- Jocelyne Eberstein - Stress is NOT Sexy
- Dr. Elena Eustache - How to Be Feminine
- Dr. Elena Eustache - The Cure for Your Broken Heart
- Susan Daya Hamwi - CALM conversation with anyone about anything
- Deborah Harper - Ascending to a New Reality
- India Holloway - Everything Begins in The Gut
- Micaela Passeri - Mastering The Roller Coaster of Life
- Michelle Perkins -You and Your Money - A Happy Couple?
- Dawn Rose - Stress and the Body-Mind Connection
- Lucie Tesarova - Avoid the Ugly Trap of Setting Flat Goals
- Mellissa Tong - How to Apply Storytelling In Marketing?
- Cheryl Walker - Family and Systemic Constellations

If you are interested in learning more about the body mind spirit connection pick up a copy of this Itty Bitty® book today, meet our authors and expand your knowledge.

Your Amazing Itty Bitty® Holistic Experts Compilation Book

15 Chapters by Holistic Professionals Who Share Fundamental Information on Areas of Their Expertise

Winifred Adams
April Braswell
Chantalynn
Jocelyne Eberstein,
 L.Ac. O.M.D.
Dr. Elena Eustache
(2 Chapters)
Susan Daya Hamwi
Deborah Harper

India Holloway
Micaela Passeri
Michelle M Perkins,
 MBA
Dawn Rose
Lucie Tesarova
Mellissa Tong
Cheryl Walker

Published by Itty Bitty® Publishing
A subsidiary of S & P Productions, Inc.

Copyright © 2020 **S &P Productions, Inc**

Treble Clef icon resource from Dreamstime.com
Roller Coaster icon resource from Flaticon.com

Printed in the United States of America

Itty Bitty Publishing
311 Main Street, Suite D
El Segundo, CA 90245
(310) 640-8885

ISBN: 978-1-950326-64-8

Dedication Page

Winifred Adams: This chapter is dedicated to all those who 'know' from the inside out and all those who were considered 'weird' as a child, but instead have a heart of gold.

April Braswell: To Jordan, who fulfilled the promise from long ago when you came into my life.

Chantalynn: I dedicate this chapter to my son, Cy. He really inspires me to be my best AND he makes my heart sing!

Jocelyne Eberstein, L.Ac. O.M.D.: This chapter is dedicated to those who choose to be agents of change for a healthier world.

Dr. Elana Eustache: I dedicate these 2 Chapters to God—Jesus - El Shadai, the God of breakthroughs. Without you, I am nothing. Through you, I am everything.
I also dedicate these chapters to my son Joshua, my parents, my two sisters and lovely Brother. Thank you all for Your love and Support .

Susan Daya Hamwi: To all my Teachers who remind me that Life is Magical and all is possible through self-love, discipline, and compassion.

Deborah Harper: To my son, who I love with all of my heart, and to all of the other great teachers in my Life.

India Holloway: This book is dedicated to the Men and Women in Uniform, our First Responders.

Micaela Passeri: To all the dreamers out there who dare to envision a life of joy, abundance, peace, happiness and flow, and go out and create it.

Michelle M Perkins MBA: I dedicate this chapter to my loving parents, creative husband, and my extraordinary kids, who expand my beliefs about what is possible.

Dawn Rose: This is dedicated to all beings on the journey of vitality, healing and happiness.

Lucie Tesarova: This short goal-setting chapter is dedicated to all of you who are done settling for less and are ready to improve the quality of your life and business. Trust the process, apply what you learned, and new exciting and more satisfying results will start showing up in your life and business!

Mellissa Tong: To my grandmother who showed me what maternal love was.

Cheryl Walker: For mom, who risked her life to give birth to me. In her death, we gave birth to our newfound freedom.

Stop by our Itty Bitty® website Directory
to find interesting information
from our experts.

www.IttyBittyPublishing.com

Or visit our Experts at:

Winifred Adams -
https://associationofmedicalintuitives.com

April Braswell –
AprilBraswell.com

Chantalynn –
www.chantalynn.com

Dr. Elena Eustache –
@Dr_elenaeustache_ (Instagram)
DrElenaeustache@yahoo.com

Jocelyne Eberstein –
www.ecenterwellness.com

Susan Daya Hamwi -
www.settlementworks.com

Deborah Harper –
www.alifeofloveandbalance.com

India Holloway –
www.HealthyLivingStudios.com

Micaela Passeri –
www.YourEQ.Info

Michelle M Perkins MBA –
Michelle@limitfreelife.com

Dawn Rose –
groundedhearthealing.com

Lucie Tesarova –
www.talkwithlucie.com

Mellissa Tong-
rockstaroncamera.com

Cheryl Walker –
www.artistsholistichouse.com

Table of Contents

Introduction

The experts in this book are truly dedicated and heart-centered professionals. Each author in the following chapters has been vetted by our peers in the holistic community. I am so honored to be a part of this amazing network. We get so much joy and pleasure in helping others thrive in these times, AND it is what we are meant to do. Please enjoy the gold that is offered here. This has been a labor of love and a long time coming yet the wisdom in these 15 chapters is timeless and most definitely timely. We wish you a beautiful journey to a thriving life with much great Health, great Wealth, and Happy-ness!

Chantalynn
Holistic Wellness & Lifestyle Influencer
Community Builder

Expert 1
Winifred Adams
The Secret Behind Medical Intuition

No human being is symptom-free. But some human beings are capable of seeing into a human body to find the energetic origin of a symptom whether the symptom is yet expressed or forthcoming. This is the field of Medical Intuition. Seeing inside a human body is like:

1. An array of colors
2. Can actually be a feeling
3. Is a knowingness or a deep conviction

The Global Association of Medical Intuitives (GAMI) is the leading association worldwide, with the latest in the field of Medical Intuition. GAMI-approved schools graduate the best medical intuitives in the world, setting the standard for professionals and students alike.

1. GAMI is leading the way to combine medical intuitives with the medical world.
2. The GAMI community fosters a dynamic environment for both the professional medical intuitive as well as those already in the medical field looking to hone their medical intuitive skills.

What You Need To Know To Become A Medical Intuitive

- Create inner trust by listening to the small voice within, the first time.
- Let go of fear and doubt by breathing deeply and relinquishing control.
- Foster patience by learning to wait until the answer comes.
- Learn the art of contemplation so that insights are more readily available.
- Regularly spend time in nature to connect and ground.
- Practicing yoga or Chi Qong is a way to feel the flow of energy both within and without (outside) your body so you can readily see this in others.
- Let go of the need to know; instead, allow and be still.
- Study with a trained professional.
- Join GAMI today! Find out more at: https://associationofmedicalintuitives.com

Expert 2
April Braswell
Soul Essence Love

If you're looking for love from a Holistic perspective, the following Dating Tips alone won't draw the kind of Soul Essence Love you seek. You risk feeling frustrated. Sure, you'll meet great people, but your Soul will continue to yearn for something more. Does that sound like you?

1. You'll go on Dates, but the connection won't be fulfilling.
2. You'll enjoy your Life and Work, but feel like something's missing.
3. Your Soul will yearn and pull you to seek your Soul Essence Mate.

It's not your fault. There is a solution! Read on to learn what to do...

What Is Soul Essence Love?

Soul Essence Love is more than just any Love Relationship. In Soul Essence Love, you and your Soul Essence Mate have aligned Life Purposes. Your work may be different, but your careers and Life Purpose Work will be aligned.

Action without Spirit: Unfulfilling Dates

You might find singles to date and do pretty well socially, but you'll always feel like something's missing. Your Soul Essence will feel unfilled. The actions will feel productive, but cut off from your Soul Essence.

- First Dates and more may happen.
- The interactions won't lead anywhere lasting.

Connecting Spiritually without Dating: No Relationship Manifested

You might connect with your Soul Essence Mate spiritually during your Prayer and Meditation time, but the person hasn't yet appeared.

- Spiritual Connection must be followed up with Positive Dating and active socializing.
- Spiritual Connection together with Positive Dating actively attracts your Soul Essence Love.

Discover what are the **10 Steps to Attract Soul Essence Love**: AprilBraswell.com/soul/.

Expert 3
Chantalynn
What Makes Your Heart Sing?

How do we live with more **Passion**, **Enthusiasm**, and **Love**? **Even** right **now**? You cut out the blame and shame. You let go of all the things that weigh you down. What to **DO** instead? Have a lot of **FUN** cultivating Self Awareness and Self Love. **Let us Celebrate your wins! Let the Heart be the Master** and let the Mind be the servant to serve all of your Heart's desires. You can live a life full of **Magic** and **Limitless** opportunities!

A few suggestions below: (Kids, please do try this at home!)

1. What do you love about your life right now? What are you grateful for?
2. What you focus on expands; so what would you like to invite more of?
3. What do you need to let go of?
4. Look at yourself with **Love** and **Compassion** and release the things that no longer serve you.
5. Where were you last year? 5 years ago? 10 years ago?
6. What has been working for you?
7. What excites you?
8. What can you celebrate?

It is not only about thinking happy thoughts…

- When you are in complete alignment with what is going on in your life, you experience fulfillment.
- It is not a thought process.
- It is more of an involuntary reflex.
- It is a natural primal response.
- The brain is not telling you to be happy. You would simply **Be Happy**.

How do you maximize and optimize your potential? You need to embrace what is and ask yourself, "How can I make it better?" You tell yourself that you get to enjoy the process.

FUN and **PLAY** are essential parts of your daily lives. And this kids, is **"What Makes Your Heart Sing!"**

I am here for you and it would be my honor to offer you unconditional Love and Support!

Expert 4
Jocelyne Eberstein
Stress Is NOT Sexy

I've Seen it All. Stress is NOT Sexy!
Stress makes you fat, stress makes you dumb,
stress makes you clumsy, stress makes you dread
the bathroom, stress makes hormones go crazy,
stress makes you aggressive, emotional, anxious
and depressed.

According to the **American** Psychological
Association, **stress** is linked to the six **leading
causes** of death: heart **disease**, cancer, lung
ailments, accidents, liver disease, and suicide.
More than 75 percent of all physician office visits
are for stress-related ailments and complaints.

Seven Scary Signs of Stress:
1. Weight and appetite, cravings out of control?
2. Headaches? Not normal…at all
3. Chronic pain: Neck, Back, Shoulders, you name it…
4. Irritability, Insomnia, Dysfunctional Sleep,
5. Fatigue, exhaustion, brain fog?
6. Digestion: gas, bloat, constipation/diarrhea?
7. Low, or worse, NO SEX DRIVE?
   One or more signs?

STOP STRESS IN IT'S TRACKS
THESE COST NOTHING!!!

- **Sleep**: Lack of sleep makes you hunt for the junk - fat, ugly and unhealthy. 7-9 hours of restful sleep minimum! You can't make it up on weekends…
- **Breathing**: Take one minute hourly – set your timer - focus on your breathing. Four counts in, four counts out.
- **Mindfulness**: Stop the mental masturbation! 3-5 minutes daily: immerse yourself in music, lose yourself in nature, breathe, walk, take a long bath or shower.
- **Movement**: No gym required. Use stairs, walk your lunch (smoothie, protein shake or water), clean the house, hike. 10 minutes or more daily.
- **Laughter**: Do one fun thing daily!
- **Food**: Protein and healthy fats are your best friends, eat them first. Everything else IS a condiment!
- **Last but not least drink water!!!!:** It oxygenates the brain, Drinking enough water it makes you pee, which makes you move, hence time to breathe.

Expert 5
Dr. Elena Eustache
How To Be Feminine

People often think that "being feminine" is something that women are just born knowing how to do. But nothing could be further from the truth! Tapping into your feminine energy replenishes you and brings you joy; it invites balance back into your life and keeps you feeling younger. However, you can't access this energy until you learn exactly what it is. In order to harness the power of femininity, you must first:

1. Make the decision to embrace your feminine nature
2. Understand that the polarity between masculine and feminine energy is what keeps relationships alive
3. Realize that feminine energy is receptive; over giving is masculine and will deplete you if you don't take time to recharge yourself
4. Learn that switching from your work persona (usually masculine) into your personal life (feminine) requires practice and a commitment to self-care.

There's a reason why you were born as a feminine being in this lifetime! So don't be afraid to celebrate, cherish and nurture your femininity.

Embracing your femininity will change your entire outlook on life.

Being in touch with your femininity means:

- Honoring your own feelings
- Saying no when it's appropriate
- Being respectful of others and emotionally stable
- Maintaining clear, healthy boundaries
- Refusing to compromise yourself or your standards to please someone else.

A healthy feminine woman is respectful and kind. But she's no doormat. She knows that self-care is the key to maintaining a balanced life. If you want to be a healthy feminine woman, you must:

- Prioritize your emotional health
- Do a minimum of three things every day that will bring you joy
- Cultivate a network of people who will love, support and encourage your greatness.

Table of Contents

stache
Broken Heart

ne experiences the
ntense grief can
meaningless.
art is the only way to
y back into your life
he Cure for Your
simple steps that will
heart fully, and in a

ger than ever
to heal

e action and inaction
honestly, for what it is
p
d surround yourself with

no have hurt you
fe
re!

uffer through years of
process can show you how
n. It will leave you
u don't drag your past
onships.

love

Love is a decision, not a feeling...

Make the decision to fully heal after a breakup. Don't just quickly move on to the next relationship, assuming that someone else is going to come along and fix the pain inside you. Only you can do that! You must be willing to ask yourself some difficult questions, like:

- How am I responsible for this situation?
- What was my part in creating it?
- How can I create healthy boundaries and expectations for my relationships in the future?
- What can I do to practice loving myself more?

Doing this work will allow you to give unconditional love far beyond anything you've ever known. You'll also be able to accept the same kind of passionate love in return. But balance and harmony can only be restored when you choose to release the pain of your past.

- Healing your heart means loving yourself
- Affirm that you're stronger than ever— then go out and live your authentic truth!

12

Expert 7
Susan Daya Hamwi
CALM Conversation With Anyone
About Anything

In this world of differing perspectives and polarized viewpoints, it may often be challenging to maintain calm and compassionate communication. There are four easy CALM method steps to support you in communicating.

1. CONNECT
2. ASK
3. LISTEN
4. MIRROR

These 4 steps help to create an energetic space to foster a constructive conversation without allowing it to break down. This is done through awareness, respectful dialogue, and discussion which restores a sense of understanding and commonality.

This method does take discipline and practice. It's important to be compassionate toward yourself and the other person. Be present - make sure to be aware of the tone of your voice and be truly curious and non-judgmental, as well as sensitive and inquisitive.

Ways to Be CALM- and Communicate Effectively

CONNECT:
- Say why the relationship is important
- Acknowledge past discussion or difficulties
- Ask if you are willing to try again
- The goal is to connect not convince
- On repeat rounds, acknowledge progress, challenges
- Be honest with "what's so."

ASK:
- Open ended questions
- Be curious, don't interrogate
- Ask about source materials
- Ask about underlying values
- Agree to mutual fact-finding missions.

LISTEN:
- and Pay close attention
- Listen to understand, not to respond
- Listen for commonalities
- Remember to BREATHE!

MIRROR:
- Paraphrase what you heard
- Acknowledge emotions and values.

When the other person is heard and understood, you can switch roles.

Expert 8
Deborah Harper
Ascending To A New Reality

This unprecedented time of change ushers in the opportunity to reflect on what we believe and how we are showing up. You have been and are continuously conditioned and programmed by:
1. Your parents and siblings
2. Teachers, leaders, religions and government
3. Social media and mainstream media

You are in the midst of the Great Awakening, or Ascension process. You role is to deprogram the mind body and stop reinforcing the programs that are running the subconscious mind. The future of Humanity depends on you doing your inner work. Remember you are powerful beings-embody it!
1. Lessen judgment of ourselves and others
2. Maintain a state of neutrality
3. Increase love and acceptance of yourself and others.

When emotions such as fear and anger take over and run the body, higher consciousness and expanded awareness is cut off, leaving the person stuck in a negative feedback loop that can be very destructive.

Here are a few steps to help you start to recognize and loosen up the programmed beliefs running in your operating system.

- Increase awareness of your emotional triggers. Make it a practice to take a mindful pause before responding, lessen judgment, and to maintain neutrality.
- Create a mindfulness/meditation practice that includes heart focused breathing to get yourself into a state of coherence, and awareness in the present moment.
- Enjoy a lifestyle that includes spending time in nature and exercise tend to release stress and help build your immune system.
- Devote time to positive books/videos and movies that expand your awareness.
- Reframe your internal narrative with expanded empowering beliefs.
- Hire a coach to help you heal your inner child and turn your inner critic to your inner cheerleader.

Expert 9
India Holloway
Everything Begins In The Gut

You are taught that disease care is done with medications and over the counter drugs. On the contrary, The body has only one job and that is to heal itself.

1. "Manage your health not your disease." To improve your body eat a healthy diet to improve your health.
2. The body is designed to clean itself. If you continue to pollute it, it will slowly die. Eat healthy foods, not dead or processed foods.
3. Your body will forgive you for everything you ever tried to do to kill it. But don't wait till it's too late and it starts to break down faster than it can heal itself.
4. It all starts in the digestive system where 100 percent of your nutrients are absorbed into your blood stream. Take in the proper nutrients to improve your health by improving your immune system.

Seven key things to know about your Gut

- The Gut is the Key to healing the body.
- If your Gut is sick and nasty, your body is slowly dying. Listen to your gut. If your Gut feels bad, fix it! Do not cover it up or disguise it with drugs.
- Remember Health and Sickness both have their roots in the Gut.
- Seventy to eighty percent of your immune system is in the Gut. Keep it clean and free flowing.
- Your Gut is one of seven pathways to get rid of waste. Eat plenty of fiber daily.
- Never eat simple carbs and animal protein together.
- Cleansing is the perfect opportunity to begin a healthy lifestyle…Naturally.

Expert 10
Micaela Passeri
Mastering The Roller Coaster Of Life

You have been riding the roller coaster of life. How has it been going? Over it? If your answer is YES, then keep reading!

You are an emotional being and life throws a lot at us, so how can you master life so your experiences are filled with more love, more abundance, more life?

By bringing more awareness to your everyday actions and reactions. Yep, it's that simple. Everyone can do it, but most won't. So here are 3 easy steps you can do every day:

1. Bring **Awareness** to each thought, intention and action; **Ask WHY.**
2. **Trust** Everything is Happening for a **Purpose.**
3. **Keep Going**, Never Give Up.

I know you've heard it before, but the key to mastery is to know yourself. To know yourself you must ask and answer the following questions:

1. What Do I Love?
2. What Makes Me Happy?
3. What is My Purpose?

What makes you Feel Good is the path to Mastery

- Look for the Next Better Feeling Place
- Be Courageous and Go For It
- See Yourself on the Other Side

Now in order to get clear on where the next better feeling place is you must get clear on your purpose and ultimately what kind of life you want to lead. From there you ask yourself:

- What is the call I am answering?
- What will it require of me?
- What is the inspired action I will take in order to fulfill it?
- What am I willing to give up to actualize it?
- How committed am I to see this through?

Lots to think about right! If you want help, I am here for you!

Expert 11
Michelle M Perkins MBA
You And Your Money - A Happy Couple?

Money advice is everywhere, yet practical
counsel can only help us if we have a healthy
partnership with money. Are you aware that you
are in a long term relationship with money?

Money relationships are complex and emotional
(just like other relationships). They originate
early, formed by money messages from those
around you. Resulting ideas drive future behavior
but don't always serve your best interests or well-
being.

Uncovering these hidden (unconscious) money
beliefs will lead to:
1. Changing the way you feel about money,
    allowing you to make more intentional,
    wiser money decisions.
2. Improving your sense of worth and
    allowing you to earn more, and keep
    more money.
3. Empowering your money mindset -
    enabling you to take control of your
    finances and build real wealth, stability
    and freedom.

To create a conflict-free kinship with money for a lifetime of benefits, start to:

- Pay attention to your money. Spend quality time with it, and learn what you have, where it comes from and where it goes.
- Become aware of spending habits and your automatic responses to financial decisions.
- Observe your thoughts about money, positive and negative, and track these thoughts for a week in a journal.
- Recognize where the thoughts come from, have they been passed down to you or do they come from your own experience?
- Identify where you lack money boundaries in some areas, perhaps giving it away or overspending because you feel guilt, shame or you want to be liked.
- Question whether you are paid what you are worth.
- Note current money challenges and how your beliefs are influencing them. Get additional support at: www.limitfreelife.com

Expert 12
Dawn Rose
STRESS AND THE MIND-BODY CONNECTION

Stress is rampant in today's modern world. You have a very busy lifestyle with many demands from work and relationships. Stress contributes to most of the illnesses you experience, indicative of the mind-body connection. Negative emotions set up shop in the body and can create a host of health issues. The results of unmanaged stress can include:

1. Anxiety and Depression
2. Chronic pain and inflammation
3. Adrenal Burnout/Fatigue

Holistic health care, such as Energy Medicine is a gentle and effective way to foster relaxation and support through the many demands of life, bringing you joy and vitality. In my practice, I offer two energy medicine modalities, Transpersonal Energy Healing and Bach Flower Therapy. Helping clients with:

1. emotional wellness,
2. spiritual growth,
3. deep relaxation,
4. and healing.

Benefits of Energy Medicine Include:

- Getting to the root cause of disharmony
- Release of limiting beliefs
- Restoring balance to your energy system
- Relaxation of your nervous system
- Enjoying less negativity/More positivity

To learn more about Energy Medicine go to
www.groundedhearthealing.com

Expert 13
Lucie Tesarova
Avoid The Ugly Trap Of Setting Flat Goals

Have you ever worked hard to accomplish your big goal, and once you finally did it, you realized it was not fulfilling?

Or you set your goal, but something always seems to be in the way of you achieving it? Perhaps you have had that goal for a long time, but it seems no matter what you do, it is not happening, and you are not getting the results that you want?

BEWARE of the **danger of setting FLAT goals** that may result in falling flat in the key areas of your life including:
1. Not achieving your goals
2. Not enjoying your results
3. Being stuck & feeling lost
4. Chasing the wrong goals

BE AWARE to **set 4D Goals** instead, leading to setting not just some goals, but the RIGHT goals – creating more:
1. Results
2. Fulfillment and joy in your life
3. Holistic success (not only healthy business but, also a healthy life)

How to set the RIGHT goals, not just "some goals."

- Pick an area of your goal (work, health, relationships, etc.).
- Get a pen and a piece of paper or open a program to type into on your phone or computer.

Ready? Set aside at least 10 minutes to answer the four questions below. Practice this exercise to set yourself up for **multi-dimensional success.**

- How do you want to **feel/be** in this area of your life/business?
- What do you want to **have** in this area of your life/business?
- What kind of **actions** do you need/want to take that would align with what you want to have and how you want to feel?
- What kind of **legacy** will you leave through accomplishing this goal?

Expert 14
Mellissa Tong
How To Apply Storytelling In Marketing?

Before you figure out how to market and differentiate yourself from your competitors, you need to first understand why your customers buy.

1. They buy because they believe your product or service is helping them with an on-going challenge that they have. Understanding this fundamental concept will help you decide what to say in front of your potential client.

2. It's never about the how, it's always about the transformation and results your client get from working with you.

Storytelling is the best way to create the emotional connection between you and your clients and get your message across. Facts are useful; you use facts to justify why you buy after you buy, but facts alone can never make your customers buy.

Here are three tips on how you can use storytelling to communicate and market yourself, especially in an elevator pitch.

Tips to Communicate and Market Yourself

- *Crafting an engaging message.* Don't just tell your potential clients what you do, tell them why you do what you do. Your why is the driving force behind every action you take and every decision you make in your business. Use that as a differentiator. Don't confuse your why with a more flexible schedule or the ability to make more money, those are results of your why, not your why.
- *Stories sell.* Our attention span has dropped to only 7 seconds. Share a success story with your audience about some of the benefits your client gets from working with you. When you tell a story, people can relate. When people can relate, they are engaged. When they are engaged, they are *actually* listening.
- *Be clear and simple with your message.* Make it easy for your customers to understand your offer. Do not get technical and try to explain things that are too complicated. A confused mind never buys. And remember, not every client is an ideal client. It's okay to let the wrong client go, so you can make room for new ones.

Step 15
Cheryl Walker
Family And Systemic Constellations:
How To Heal Generational Programming

You can't change your ancestry, but you can change your awareness of the self-limiting behaviors you unconsciously inherited from your ancestors. Your relationships with family members, living or dead, affect all the personal and professional relationships in your life, as well as your relationship to yourself.

When you become aware of your unconscious behaviors, or **blind spots**, you can consciously change the direction of your life.

Family Constellations create space for making the unconscious conscious so that you can course correct and re-adjust the GPS for your own life direction.

Family Constellations:
1. Speak the unspoken
2. Acknowledge the unacknowledged
3. Include the excluded
4. Restore balance and belonging

What's your emotional inheritance?

- Have you ever felt invisible? Ashamed? Left out? Not good enough? Powerless?
- Do you have health issues? Addictions?
- Have you experienced a loss? A death? A divorce? A job loss? An accident?
- Are you at a crossroads in your life?
- Do you hate your job or your boss?
- Are you a victim of circumstance?
- Have you experienced episodes or prolonged periods of depression?
- Do you struggle in relationships?
- Do you often feel overwhelmed?
- Have you experienced isolation?
- Have you experienced trauma?
- Do you have an inner critic?
- Have you ever felt silenced?
- Do you have family secrets?

If you answered **YES** to any of these questions, **Family Constellations** can change your life.

You've finished. Before you go…

Tweet/share that you finished this book.

Please star rate this book.

Reviews are solid gold to writers. Please take a few minutes to give us some itty bitty feedback.

ABOUT THE AUTHORS

Winifred Adams-Winifred Adams is a Medical Intuitive/Master Healer and Founder/President of the Global Association of Medical Intuitives. She is a best-selling author and Founder of Making Life Brighter.

April Braswell - America's Midlife Dating Coach, award winning expert, April Braswell is the Midlife Dating columnist at www.DatingAdvice.com. Her mission is to empower and equip men and women to find, attract, and nourish the Lifelong Love they seek via speaking, coaching and Home Study Courses

Chantalynn- is a Holistic Wellness & Lifestyle Influencer, a Community Builder, and a busy "Mompreneur" with an appetite for Life! She is also the President of the Santa Monica Chapter of the Holistic Chamber of Commerce.

Dr. Elena Eustache - Dr. Elena Eustache, founder of the Eustache Institute and also known as the Encyclopedia of Love, has a Ph.D. in Psychology and Cognitive Behavior Therapy. In addition to being a relationship expert to today's hottest celebrities, athletes, politicians, royalty, and people from all walks of life, Dr. Eustache is the Executive Producer and host of The Dr. Elena Eustache Show on Instagram, where she interviews celebrities and influencers, and provides daily love tips to over 150 thousand followers. Dr. Eustache is also the author of the successful self-help book titled, The Cure for your Broken Heart, which can be found on <u>Amazon.com</u> along with her new book, How to be feminine. She is also the founder and creator of LoveTheApp, an online dating platform to find true love, commitment or marriage

Jocelyne Eberstein-is the founder of the eCenter in Los Angeles, CA, a Licensed Acupuncturist, Doctor of Oriental Medicine, Functional Medicine Board Eligible, and she also holds a B.S. in Nuclear Medicine Technology. Her distinctive incorporation of evidence-based science and techniques along with eastern wisdom as well as her training, experience and creativity have led her to develop systems and strategies that provide real, measurable health breakthroughs for her patients around the world.

Susan Daya Hamwi-blends her gifts as a family lawyer, mediator, and kundalini yogi to provide a safe supportive space for dynamic family resolution. Her clients emerge from the process with dignity, self empowerment, self respect as they co-create solutions together.

Deborah Harper- is a Certified Professional Coach, Speaker and Trainer. She has a master's certification in transition dynamics.

India Holloway- National Board Certified Colon HydroTherapist, Iridologist, Lecturer and Author

of the Book: "The Body Doesn't Know How
to Die"

Micaela Passeri- is an Award winning
Emotional Intelligence and Business Performance
Expert, International Speaker, Author and
Community Leader. Entrepreneurial and
business women hire her to identify and release
the trapped emotions that halt their money flow
and success and help them transform from stuck,
stagnant and unfulfilled to happy,
liberated, hopeful and healed.

Michelle M Perkins MBA- Fulfillment,
enjoyment and growth through work are key
contributors to a successful life. Michelle M.
Perkins, a former CPA and business consultant
turned executive career transition and business
strategy coach, is passionate about helping men
and women to create work they love and freedom
in their lives.

Dawn Rose- has been in the healing arts for over
15 years and is the owner of Grounded Heart,
Holistic Healing for Women in Mar Vista, CA.

Lucie Tesarova, MA, BCC - is a board-certified
personal and business coach and the founder of
Consult to Success, a coaching and consulting
firm. Her mission is to empower and equip others
with tools to create fulfilling experiences and
results in their personal and professional lives,
through her company's coaching and consulting
services.

Mellissa Tong- Is an Amazon #1 best-selling author, speaker, and award-winning storyteller. She works with Fortune 500s and B2B companies on crafting compelling messages and engaging visual stories to get their customers buying.

Cheryl Walker- Through Family Constellations Cheryl Walker has healed her relationship with her father and emerged from a life in black and white to a life in full Technicolor.

If you enjoyed this Itty Bitty® Book you might also like…

- **Your Amazing Itty Bitty® Business Experts Compilation Book** – Various Authors

- **Your Amazing Itty Bitty® Book of Words**– Various Authors

- **Your Amazing Itty Bitty® Health And Wellness Experts Compilation Book** – Various Authors

And many other Itty Bitty® Books available on line at www.ittybittypublishing.com

Made in the USA
Coppell, TX
05 December 2020

43104584R00028